IN-LAWS, OUTLAWS

BUILDING
BETTER RELATIONSHIPS

In-Laws, Outlaws
Building
Better Relationships

by

Norman Wright

Harvest House Publishers
Irvine, California 92714

IN-LAWS, OUTLAWS

Copyright © 1977 Harvest House Publishers
Irvine, California 92714
Library of Congress Catalog Card Number:
   77-82036
ISBN 0-89081-079-6

Printed in the United States of America

CONTENTS

1

In-Laws Or Out-Laws?

The couple sat silently for several minutes. Finally, the young wife blurted out, "I've put up with it for four years and I've had it! I am sick and tired of the triangle! Only with him, the other woman is his mother. And unless you can help us, our marriage is finished!"

Before I could say a word, she took a breath and started in listing the reasons why she felt like she did. "Tony's mother calls him every day. Never fails! If I answer the phone, she simply asks for Tony and then waits silently. I can't even get her to talk to me. Whenever she comes over to the house, she starts listing all the things that are wrong. 'Why can't the kids do this or that.' To her, everything's my fault. I'm not raising the kids right. I'm not treating Tony like a good wife should. Everything I do is wrong, according to her. And just because I'm not Italian, she refers to me as her 'foreign daughter-in-law.' And he just lets it go on and on. I don't get any support from him. Some husband I've got!'' With that remark, she folded her arms and glared at her husband.

Tony sat there looking at the floor. When it appeared he wasn't going to say anything, I finally asked him, ''Well, Tony, how do you feel about what Joyce has just told me?''

It seemed like forever before he looked up and started talking. I noticed tears in his eyes. ''What can I do?'' he pleaded. ''I want my marriage to work, but I don't want to hurt my mom. Everything Joyce said is true, but Mom has some needs too. I'm at the point where I don't know what to say or do to either one of them. Are we the only couple with these kinds of problems?''

As we talked together during that first hour,

both Tony and Joyce related their confused emotions with both sets of parents. After they left my office, I thought of the other two couples I had talked with that day who were having in-law problems. I felt like I was faced with an epidemic.

How is Your Attitude?

How do you relate to your in-laws? When someone says "mother-in-law," what thoughts or feelings spontaneously come to your mind? Do you think in-law problems are more severe today than in years past?

Here is a "quicky-quiz" you can take to evaluate your attitudes toward in-laws. It was developed by Dr. Richard Klemer[1], who has done extensive research in this area. Mark down your response to each question, and then check

1. Richard H. Klemer, Instructor's Manual to accompany Marriage and Family Relationships, prepared by Rebecca Smith (New York: Harper & Row, 1970), pp. 126-128.

the back of the book for the correct answers. The multiple choice statements may have more than one correct answer.

True or False?

1. Jokes about mothers-in-law may have a self-perpetuating effect on the mother-in-law as a problem.
2. Some people work out a better relationship with their in-laws than they do with their own parents.
3. Researchers agree that in-laws are the prime problem for newlyweds.
4. If a wife is employed outside the home, society does expect her to reach as high a standard as the wife who stays at home.
5. The competition between women who are in-laws is greater than between men who are in-laws.
6. Duvall found that there is a feminine angle in nearly all in-law problems.
7. In-law problems probably occur because the newly married couple was not ready to leave home.

8. Exaggerated independence from parents can have as devastating an effect on in-law adjustment as can overdependence.
9. Possessive parents can be as great a problem as over-dependent children.
10. Parents who have lived full, well-rounded lives make better in-laws because they are not overeager to run their children's lives.
11. As young couples grow older, the in-law problem becomes more difficult.
12. A separate household is not considered as important as it once was in fostering good in-law relations.
13. When there is friction in a family, there is often a tendency to blame the spouse's family.

Multiple Choice

1. The mother-in-law's greater involvement in marital difficulties may stem from her:
   a. Being closer to the children than the father is.
   b. Being left without the time-consuming job of rearing children.

   c. Being too near the same age as the young couple.

2. The most likely person to be part of in-law problems is the:
   a. Sister-in-law.
   b. Brother-in-law.
   c. Husband's sister.
   d. Wife's mother.
   e. Husband's mother.

3. The factor most often involved in in-law difficulty is that one of the persons is:
   a. Overdependent.
   b. Neurotic.
   c. Not satisfied in the previous stage of the family life cycle.
   d. Expressing a wait-and-see attitude.
   e. A female.

4. Parents-in-law can help the young married couple by:
   a. Leaving them completely alone.
   b. Helping when needed without placing an obligation on the gift.
   c. Leading a self-fulfilling life of their own.
   d. Taking on some of the young couple's

financial obligations.
  e. Treating them as adults.
5. The young married couple could help the in-law problem by:
  a. Becoming familiar with the problems of middle-aged parents.
  b. Allowing the in-laws to help out if they want to.
  c. Looking at both sides of the problem.
  d. Becoming familiar with the research about newlyweds.
  e. Following the norms in the methods of in-law adjustment.
6. Some factors that seem to be related to good in-law adjustment are:
  a. A church wedding that includes both sets of parents.
  b. Approval of the marriage by all parents.
  c. Friendliness of both sets of parents to each other.
  d. Happy marriages of the parents of the couple.
  e. Having children within five years.
7. The factor of dependence is involved in which

of these indicators of good in-law adjustment:
a. Approval of the couple's marriage by the parents.
b. A separate household for each of the three families.
c. Marriage between persons of the same religion.
d. Happy marriage for both sets of parents of the couple.
e. Meeting the prospective partner's family before the marriage.
8. In-law problems:
a. Are most prevalent in the first year of marriage.
b. Are more prevalent after the children come.
c. Increase as both couples get older.
d. Are more prevalent among very young couples.
e. Decrease as both couples get older.

Now that you have checked your answers against those of Dr. Klemer, do you find that your relationship reflects the findings of his research? In what areas are yours different? In what areas of your in-law relationship would you like to see some improvement?

Attitudes in Other Cultures

Many cultures have strict traditions regarding in-laws. "In more than three-fifths of the world's societies, severe penalties follow upon the meeting of a man and his mother-in-law, and they shun each other accordingly. In northern Australia, a man who speaks to his mother-in-law must be put to death. In parts of the South Pacific, both parties would commit suicide. In Yucatan, men believe that to meet one's mother-in-law face to face would render a man sterile for life, so he may travel miles out of his way over dangerous territory to avoid being near her. Navajo men believe that they will go blind if they should see their mothers-in-law, so she is not even allowed to attend the wedding."[2]

2. John M. Schlien, "Mother-in-law: A Problem in Kinship Terminology," ETC, (July 1962), pp. 161-171. Reprinted by permission from ETC: A Review of General Semantics, ©1962 by the International Society for General Semantics.

The Bible and In-Laws

What does the Bible say about in-laws? Are there any prohibitions? Do the scriptures give us any absolute guidelines concerning in-law relationships? There is nothing specific, only the basic teachings of Christian living which apply to any relationship. Biblical principles, such as living in harmony with one another; encouraging one another; being kind, forgiving, and tender-hearted; are the basis for good in-law relationships. Have you ever considered the fact that if your parents or in-laws are believers they are members of the body of Christ, and therefore they are also brothers and sisters in Christ?

The Bible does *not* say that children should have their parents live with them or that they are responsible for their parents when they are older. In fact, there are only a few direct references in the scriptures to in-law relationships. Three are mentioned here. The first is found in the Old Testament. In patriarchal times families lived in tightly knit groups or, as some would call them, clans. The young men of that time were encouraged to choose their wife from within that same clan in order to preserve the purity of its bloodline and to uphold their beliefs and ideals.

Esau was one of those who chose to marry outside the group. He chose two women, Judith and Basemath. He did not consider the desire of his group, his parents, or whether these women would make the best wives for him. They were Hittite women who had beliefs, ideals, and a religion which were very different. The record appears in Genesis 26:34-35 (Amplified): "Now Esau was 40 years old when he took as wife Judith the daughter of Berri the Hittite, and Basemath the daughter of Elon the Hittite. *And they made life bitter and a grief of mind and spirit for [their parents-in-law] Isaac and Rebekah"* [emphasis added].

Rebekah found it very difficult to adjust to these two wives with their different customs and manners. These people lived in very close contact and had to function together. Probably Rebekah's customs seemed strange to Esau's two wives. Rebekah finally exclaimed one day,

". . . I am weary of my life because of the daughters of Heth [these wives of Esau]! If Jacob takes a wife of the daughters of Heth, such as these Hittite girls around here, what good will my life be to me?" (Gen. 27:46, Amplified). Even Esau became discouraged with the disharmony in the home, so he married another woman, hoping his parents would approve and perhaps some harmony might develop as well.

Another example of an in-law relationship was Naomi and Ruth. Naomi was a different kind of mother-in-law. She was able to inspire love and devotion in Ruth to the extent that Ruth did not want to leave her: "And Ruth said, Urge me not to leave you, or to return from following you; for where you go, I will go; and where you lodge, I will lodge; your people shall be my people, and your God my God; where you die, I will die, and there will I be buried. The Lord do so to me, and more also, if anything but death parts me from you" (Ruth 1:16-17, Amplified). Positive in-law relationships occurred then as they can today.

Another positive example is seen in the life of

Moses. In Exodus 18, the story of Moses and Jethro begins with Moses literally wearing himself out with all the work and responsibility he was taking upon himself. His father-in-law came into the Israelite camp and saw that Moses had to settle every dispute. Jethro was quite direct in his suggestion to Moses (Exod. 18:13-24, Amplified):

"Next day Moses sat to judge the people, and the people stood around Moses from morning until evening. When Moses' father-in-law saw all that he was doing for the people, he said, What is this that you do for the people? Why do you sit alone, and all the people stand around you from morning till evening? Moses said to his father-in-law, Because the people come to me to inquire of God. When they have a dispute they come to me, and I judge between a man and his neighbor, and I make them know the statutes of God and His laws. Moses' father-in-law said to him, "the thing that you are doing is not good. You will surely wear out both yourself and this people with you, for the thing is too heavy for you; you are not able to perform it all by yourself. Listen now to [me], I will counsel you, and God will be with you. You shall represent the people before God, bringing their cases and causes to Him, teaching them the decrees and laws, showing them the way they must walk, and the work they must do. Moreover you shall choose able men from all the people, God-fearing men of truth, who hate unjust gain, and place them over thousands, hundreds, fifties, and tens, to be their rulers. And let them judge the people at all times; every great matter they shall bring to you, but every small matter they shall judge. So it will be easier for you, and they will bear the burden with you. If you will do this, and God so commands you, you will be able to endure [the strain], and all this people also will go to their [tents] in peace. *So Moses listened to and heeded the voice of his father-in-law, and did all that he had said"* [emphasis added].

If that kind of situation had occurred in your life, how would you have responded? Would you listen to, weigh, and evaluate the advice of your in-laws before responding? The advice may represent years of wisdom and experience which could save you time, effort, and even money! Jethro's advice was not given because he was meddling. He was concerned for Moses and for the people. He wanted Moses to be able to use his gifts to the best advantage for him and for the people.

In-law relationships have had a mixed history. Are there any indications that the problems are more severe today? Let's look at some of the pressures on families and parents today.

2

Most Mothers
Become Mothers-In-Law

The strong emphasis upon independence has weakened some of the traditional family ties in our present American culture. This creates new and different pressures for the family. As a result, there seems to be a growing concern with the quality of interpersonal relationships within the family. Parents and their married children are both sensitive to the effects of meddling, interference, and overdependence.

In spite of this, problems still occur. Many young people enter marriage eager to break away from a physical dependence upon their parents, but are unable to break their emotional dependence. The resulting conflict is intensified by society's expectation that married people be independent of their parents. When this conflict is unresolved, the young person feels a growing competition between his spouse, the spouse's parents and his own parents.

For many newlyweds, marriage is the first real opportunity to experience a feeling of independence. Any real, or presumed threat to this independence is seen as someone forcing them to remain a child. So the young person usually overreacts to any suggestions from the parent.

The Pain of Letting Go

Many parents have difficulty at this time for they do not want to let go of their child. Parents who have been accustomed to having their child depend on them for twenty years have mixed feelings about handing over that relationship to someone else. These feelings are mixed with a genuine concern for the welfare of their child, as well. Even though many would not admit it, both parents and their offspring are a bit reluctant to let go of each other.

This is especially true of those who have grown up in what is called a *depressogenic* environment. In this kind of home atmosphere, an individual is not allowed to develop or express any sense of independence. Either one or both of the parents seek to maintain continual control over their growing child. These parents fear that their teenager will make a wrong decision or mar the family reputation. They refuse to allow the young man or woman to become a self-sustaining, independent person, able to make mature decisions based on a personal set of internalized values.

The parents who create this depressogenic environment were probably often not allowed to develop their own feelings of independence when they were adolescents. Usually, these adults also have a very low opinion of themselves, which in turn fosters a low self-image in their children. When a child seeks to assert his own self, these parents will disregard the feelings of the child and force him to conform to the image the parents have of that child. If the young person then continues to try and express his true feelings, he is overwhelmed with feelings of guilt, which only feed the very system that fosters a poor self-image.

If you grew up in this kind of atmosphere, you have had a difficult time establishing your independence. You may still be struggling to break free from your parents. Or, if you have made a radical break from them, you may still be trying to learn how to live on your own with confidence.

This depressogenic environment can also be seen in the home where one person is encouraged to be dependent upon another member of the family, such as a brother, sister, or an aunt. This person is made to feel as if he cannot possibly survive without the other's emotional support. He cannot make decisions without the other persons advice and involvement. We are all dependent upon others to some degree, but this type of dependence is unhealthy. Even though another person may foster this type of dependence in a home, it takes the cooperation of each person to perpetuate this type of relationship.

Of course, this continued dependency deeply affects the new relationship with a spouse. The dependent partner may still be trying to win his or her parents' praise and approval. However, your value and worth do *not* depend upon your parents' approval. Their standards may be so unrealistic and unattainable that no one, even they themselves, could possibly measure up.

The way you respond to your parents or to your in-laws may still be linked to the kind of parent you had as you were growing up. Consider these specific types[3] of parents and see if you can identify with any of them.

Perfectionistic Parents

Some parents are *perfectionists*. They tend to reject things their children do no matter how well they achieve. Regardless of the level of

3. Adapted from Thomas D. Gnagey, How to Put up with Parents (Champaign, Ill.: Research Press, 1975), pp. 82-91.

expertise a child attains, there is continual criticism. This type of parent believes something can always be done better and fails to offer any praise or encouragement for what is attained. Unfortunately, this pattern does not change when the child leaves home or is married.

Criticism can either be overt or implied through patterns of speech or nonverbal communication. Children learn to respond with feelings of guilt, frustration, and unhappiness. This continues until they learn that it is useless to try to live up to their parents' expectations, since they can never be met. It is not our responsibility to always seek to please our parents. We need to remind ourselves that it is okay not to be perfect. Perhaps we can convey this to our parents as we accept imperfection from them. After all, we are all imperfect. Learn to accept and appreciate their weaknesses as these make them more human and even more lovable.

When you receive criticism from this type of parent after you are married you will be tempted to become very defensive, extremely angry, or even want to tell them to get lost. However, none of these responses will solve the problem. A response that might help when you get criticism is, "I'm sorry that you're unhappy with what I have done or am doing, but I rather like it myself." Or, "What I am doing is just for my own enjoyment and whether it is perfect or not I like it." Or, you might say, "What I think you are saying is that I didn't quite do it the way you expected. You're right, but I feel good about the way it is coming out." Whenever this type of parent (or in-law) gives you a compliment, it is important that you respond in a positive manner: "Thanks for the compliment. I appreciate your noticing that."

Rejecting Parents

Other parents are called *rejecting* parents. Their rejection comes not from anything that you have done. There needs to be no apparent reason at all. Rejection can be demonstrated by withholding love, and can even go to the point of taking out hostilities against you in a physical manner. If your parents treated you this way, you probably felt isolated, lonely, and perhaps very bitter. But rejection is usually the problem of the one doing the rejecting rather than of the one being rejected.

You can learn to live as though the rejection did not exist. Look for acceptance from those who can see the value and worth within you. Your spouse, or even your in-laws, may respond to you in a much healthier manner than your own parents. Realize that they are probably much more accurate in their response to you.

Overprotective Parents

Some individuals came from homes where the parents are *overprotective*. These parents help build problems for their children. In their eagerness to protect, they deny the child the opportunity to learn to fend for himself. In some ways this parent sets up the child to come rebounding back home after he is married, especially if the new spouse tends not to be overprotective. If you came from this type of home background you may have chosen a spouse you felt you could depend upon. This may work out nicely as long as your spouse wants to be leaned on, but when he or she tires of this kind of relationship, watch out! You need to recognize this type of relationship and begin to develop your own individual strengths, independence and sense of responsibility.

Overindulgent Parents

Perhaps you came from a home dominated by an *overindulgent* parent. Instead of *doing* too much for the child, this parent *gives* too much. If you came from this type of home, you probably did not learn to postpone rewards or learn the value of working for what you want. Items were just handed to you. As a result, you may now expect this in every area of your life.

These parents usually create children who are selfish, demanding, and who feel the world owes them a living. When this attitude continues on into a marriage relationship, all kinds of trouble can develop with the spouse and the in-laws.

If you came from this type of home

environment, you need to learn to work for things yourself and discover the joy of attainment. You will also need to learn how to say no to your parents. Discuss this problem with your spouse and ask for help in becoming a more giving person instead of a getting person.

Overpermissive Parents

Then there is the *overpermissive* parent. There are few rules or guidelines in this home. If your parents are this way and your spouse's parents are not, you can easily see the potential problems. This is especially true when you decide that your home will have some rules and clear guidelines for your children's behavior. The overpermissive parent, who is now a grandparent, can undo years of training in just one week's visit. You need to stand together with your spouse to affirm what you believe.

Some parents expect daily phone calls from their married children. When they do call, these parents do nothing but complain that they haven't been phoned often enough. Sometimes both sets of parents do some cross-checking to make sure the couple is spending equal amount of time with them. Or one mother may expect a regular dinner invitation or insist on weekly visits. Other parents may demand assistance in making repairs in their home or with shopping. In each situation, time is the magic ingredient that allows the emotional dependence of the parent-child relationship to develop into the emotional give-and-take of a mature and healthy relationship.

Those who marry at a younger age will have a more difficult time striving for independence. Often they have not yet worked out their feelings and thoughts about adult responsibilities. This process must be continued after they are married so they can approach their in-laws with adult responses.

Mothers-in-Law

Each of these types of parents can intensify in-law problems for the new couple. However, most in-law conflicts appear to be between the women — the wife and his mother in particular. Take a minute and write down some ideas why you think this is true:

_____

_____

_____

_____

One writer suggested that because our society is male dominated, the women are forced to compete for the favor and attention of men. Men reinforce this dominance by encouraging this competition. The wife seeks the favor and attention of her husband, but so does his mother. Added to this competition factor is the strong emphasis placed on a woman being ''a good wife.'' In spite of the women's liberation movement, this is still true today. Much more emphasis is placed upon the woman's role than upon the man's role as a husband.

What are the consequences of this? For one thing, a bride approaches marriage wondering if she will be adequate for her new role. As soon as the honeymoon is over, competition begins with his mother. This isn't discussed openly, but the feeling is present. The young wife wonders if she can cook as well as his mother. Is the house clean enough? The competition is really unfair, for it is between a novice and one who has been meeting this man's needs for over twenty years.

Another possible reason that more pressure falls on the woman is the fact that both sets of parents are less likely to risk open conflict with the husband. They recognize that he has the power to decide to move a thousand miles away.

Others suggest that in-law problems are more acute with the women because the mother is more threatened by the marriage of a child than the father. A father's life does not revolve around the children like the mother's often does. When children grow up and get married, the mother faces a real adjustment, searching about for something to validate her life and give it meaning. The mother may also begin to sense her age. Because our society values youth, some others seek to appear young by clinging to their sons.

This process is intensified when the father

does not realize what his wife is struggling against and assist her in making an adjustment when the children leave home. Insensitivity on the part of the father-in-law may account for many of the conflicts between the mother-in-law and the daughter-in-law. But mother takes the brunt of the blame.

Another factor may simply be the different way that women express their feelings and deal with conflict. Men are more apt to involve themselves in open confrontation where the problem can either be solved or a compromise reached. Women tend to express themselves in less obvious ways. The conflict between a mother-in-law and her daughter-in-law may simmer beneath the surface. When it does come out into the open, the men may step in and take control, or simply ignore what is happening.

The potential for problems is certainly present in any in-law relationship. But do in-laws break up marriages? The truth of the matter is that in and of themselves, poor in-law relationships do not break up many marriages. Divorced people often attribute some of the blame to the in-laws, but in reality they were not the final cause of the dissolution.

Usually, the same personality traits that create or contribute to in-law problems also cause other kinds of problems within a marriage. These couples, who do not have a good relationship between themselves, will have in-law problems regardless of the kind of in-laws they have. The couple who is working on their own marital adjustments, who can openly and objectively discuss their families, and who is secure with each other, will perhaps find some in-law relationships irritating, but they will not allow them to break up their marriage.

3

The Trouble
With Children-In-Law

We've considered some of the problems created by parents in the in-law relationships. But problems can also be caused by the children. Some young couples exploit their parents financially. Whenever they run into a money problem, they run to one set of parents for help. Unfortunately, the parents who respond to this call and solve the immediate problem may only be adding to the later problems. Their motives may be good, but some parents may actually enjoy seeing the young couple running to them, for it perpetuates the dependency relationship.

". . . any amount of financial dependence on parents can provoke problems. A husband or wife getting a monthly allowance from a parent may find it hard to resist criticizing his or her spouse. A young man working for his father-in-law may feel resentful or abnormally competitive. Parents who give money often feel they should have some control over what it is used for; some unconsciously use it as a device to maintain control.

"This does not mean that temporary, limited financial help is always detrimental. It does require understanding and maturity on the part of giver and receiver. So far as the parents are concerned, giving should be done without strings attached. Both the parents and the young couple must expect that some problems will arise. Rather than pretend the problems don't exist by fearfully avoiding confrontation, they should try to work them out in frank discussion. A young couple should be cautious about accepting help. Parents and in-laws should be careful about offering it."[4]

4. Norman Lobsenz and Clark Blackburn, How to Stay Married, (New York, N.Y.: Fawcett World Library, 1972), p. 54.

Insensitivity

Problems can also be created by the young couple through insensitivity. They fail to recognize that their parents and in-laws have needs or a life of their own and either impose upon them too much for baby-sitting or ignore them by a lack of communication. It is very easy for young couples to take advantage of their in-laws.

Mobility

Other in-law problems in our culture are caused by the mobility of families. Young families move often, and when they move farther away, some in-laws feel neglected.

Adjustability

Another definite problem has been graphically described by Robert Kelly:

"Still another source of difficulty may be *the pattern of give-and-take in family life.* Life begins as parents take full responsibility for our initial steps in life. They feed us, clothe us, shelter us, protect us, and often pamper us. In almost every American middle- or upper-class family, children grow up with fond expectations of many generous gifts from their parents. There are toys under the Christmas tree, birthday presents, trips to the circus and the fair, vacations to the shore or the state park. There are new clothes for school in the fall, a chance to drive the family car for the big date on Friday night, or perhaps even some help to purchase a car just for the teenage son who will be a senior in high school. College years are often more of the same, with money for tuition and college expenses and perhaps even a little extra for a mid-semester or summer trip to some exotic place. American parents are used to giving tangible expressions of their love and affection to their children. In many cases, they give too much. Children do not learn to stand on their own feet, and are afraid of breaking their dependence patterns lest parental subsidies be cut off.

"In contrast, the things children give their parents are intangible. A boy is expected to do well in athletics or the Boys' Club. A girl is expected to be popular, to be chosen queen of the spring dance or secretary of her social club. Since the number of chores to be accomplished around the house seem constantly to lessen and there are few family work projects that need the aid of every child, parents are most anxious to see results from their guidance and training through the achievements of the children. As a son or daughter enters teenage years and then goes to college, these achievements bring satisfaction to the parents, although they may continue to add to their financial burdens as well.

"A question naturally arises. When do parents cease to be completely 'givers' and begin to receive appreciation and perhaps tangible aid from their grown children? When does the tide begin to flow in the reverse direction? Our culture does not major in gratitude. Will a change come at the time of marriage? No, because most young couples are not well established financially and do not feel able to be generous to others. They still are on the receiving end. When children are born to the couple? No, because once more heavy burdens of responsibility fall on the new parents. When the children are in school? Perhaps, although a large family may feel heavy pressures to maintain its own living standards without finding extra time, energy, and money for the grandparents. When the children are in college? Probably not, for financial burdens are often the heaviest here. It is easy for grown children to ignore the needs of their parents all along. They are expected to gladly yield status and authority to the younger generations.

"Finally, when the 'young people' are in their late forties or early fifties, they may really be in a position to extend tangible help to their parents. They can afford to help to furnish a new apartment, or take the folks on a nice vacation, or to make some other material expression of their lifelong gratitude and appreciation. But, after 45 years of being on the receiving end, will they really do such things? And on the other side, if the parents have come to feel that they will never be appreciated for all of their hard work and sacrifice, may they be reluctant to accept gifts and assistance? Will they be afraid of assuming new relationships in the structure of the extended family? There is often a wide gap between the actual and the ideal situation for the retired people in our society."[5]

Any new relationship will involve adjustments. That is a fact of life. So why should young couples and parents be surprised when they discover that they too will have to make adjustments? Why be surprised when conflicts seem to arise?

"Dr. Allan Fromme, in his book, *The Psychologist Looks at Love and Marriage*, indicates, 'A marriage which avoids at least occasional tension and strain as a result of the in-law situation is rare indeed. Even before they marry, many people expect some trouble of this sort. The mere mention of the matter is enough to elicit a grimace from someone who is married.' It is true that many jokes have been

5. Robert K. Kelley, <u>Courtship, Marriage and the Family</u> (New York: Harcourt Brace Jovanovich, 1969), pp. 409, 410.

made about in-laws, and many of these jokes are indicative of resentments which suggest considerable hostility and aggression on the part of individuals towards the in-laws. Dr. Evelyn Duvall, in a very fine book, *In-Laws: Pro and Con*, indicates some of the leading types of jokes directed at in-laws. Some of the jokes are quite antagonistic and negative while others tend to be positive. She lists eight leading themes of antagonism towards the American mother-in-law in current jokes:

1. Mother-in-law talks too much.
2. Knows all the answers—the wrong ones.
3. Is a meddlesome troublemaker.
4. Is an ego deflater.
5. Is mean.
6. Is a loathsome object of aggression.
7. Comes too often and stays too long.
8. Is to be avoided.

"The *New Yorker*, for example, is quoted as saying that a mother-in-law is one who has 'a heart as big as a mountain and a mouth twice the size.' . . . A Texan referred to the mother-in-law as follows: 'A mother rocks the cradle, but a mother-in-law rocks the boat.' George Murdock, an anthropologist, found that the avoidance of the mother-in-law occurs in more than half of the societies he investigated (57 per cent of 250 different societies which he studied in all parts of the world). To some degree, the difficulty with in-laws may be the result of unfavorable conditioning in early life of most children towards their mothers-in-law, and also the tendency to anticipate difficulty with in-laws is also likely to be the case. Thus, there tends to be a stereotype of negative feelings towards the mother-in-law. Duvall indicates a general hopeful feeling that negative reactions toward in-laws as a stereotyped response may be becoming less likely in American life. She says,

" 'In general, it is clear that many persons today challenge the old-fashioned mother-in-law joke as outmoded. In a day when good human relations are seen to rest upon elimination of prejudice, old stereotypes of all kinds are being challenged. The principle is being developed of seeing preference for the unique individual each is, rather than discriminating against members of a class, bearing a particular label. This factor in family relations may need the same kind of pointing up that has been required in combating various sources of group prejudices in society. This is a feeling of an unexpected number of men and women who have participated in this exploration of in-law relationships' ''[6]

When a couple marries, the hierarchy of relationships between each spouse and his or her family is changed. In order to cope successfully with these modified family relationships, a young couple must clarify their relationship to each other. *Their primary allegiance is to each other, not to his or her parents.* When the couple has clarified their relationship to each other, they can then seek out mature ways to help their relatives accept this change of roles and relationships.

6. Bernard J. Oliver, Jr., Marriage and You (New Haven, Conn.: College and University Press, 1964), pp. 210, 211; quoting Allan Fromme, The Psychologist Looks at Love and Marriage, Evelyn Duvall, In-Laws: Pro and Con, and George Murdock, Social Structure.

Other Factors

Here are the factors that influence the type and quality of relationships which can develop between couples and their in-laws. [7]

1. The ages of the couple in comparison to the ages of the parents are a possible source of conflict. The underaged couple who has not made a break from home by living elsewhere or attending college in another location is faced with *this* adjustment while at the same time being faced with the adjustment of learning to relate to another person in a marriage relationship.

If the parents are middle-aged and still involved in careers and achievements, they have interests and rewards apart from their married children. And if they have assisted their children into adulthood, they may be looking forward to responding to their children now as adults on an

7. Adapted from Richard Hunt and Edward Rydman, Creative Marriage (Boston: Holbrook Press, 1976), pp. 174-177).

equal basis. But if parents have any of the following characteristics they may demand attention from their children: A declining income, restriction in interests, chronic illness, or very old age. A divorce of one of the parents could modify the relationship as well. Are you in this category in any way? Describe the effect it has had:

_____

_____

2. The spouses' birth order in their families can influence the relationships with relatives. If one is the oldest child in a family and the other the youngest, this difference could affect their marriage relationship as well as the expectations of parents or in-laws. If one is the last child, the parents may be somewhat reluctant to let go. On the other hand, the parents of the oldest child may expect a great deal more of their son-in-law or daughter-in-law, especially if their own is a highly productive person or is achievement-oriented. Are these factors operating in your marriage or do you see their effects?
If so, what have you done to adjust to these influences? _____

3. Couples and their parents often have unrealistic expectations of what the ideal relationship should be between the parents and the married children. Before reading on, describe what you think the ideal relationship should be with your in-laws: _____

_____

Perhaps one set of parents has imagined a close continuing relationship between themselves and their new son-in-law or daughter-in-law. They assume they will get together every weekend, call every third day, and enjoy Thanksgiving and Christmas together. They are also certain that the young couple will never live more than ten miles away so they can have constant contact with their grandchildren. And they expect at least four grandchildren, the first within two years!

But what if the young couple has other plans. What if they plan on not having any children, living two thousand miles away, and writing their parents once a month? These expectations need to be openly discussed as far in advance of any changes as possible.

Another problem in the area of expectations arises when one comes from a family with close and warm relationships and the other does not. The one may not want to establish a close relationship with his in-laws. But sometimes the situation reverses itself. The person who had little or no warm close times at home will seek a close relationship with the in-laws, while the one whose family was close wants to break away! What is your relationship like in this area? What changes would you like to make?

_____

_____

_____

4. The newly married couple's choice of where to live may influence relationships with in-laws. Couples who live with parents are only asking for increased conflicts.

"Living with parents or in-laws is almost always a bad idea. It gives the parents too much opportunity to act out their natural feelings that the 'young people' aren't grown up enough to know what's best for them. The young couple are (or feel) restricted in many ways. Often their sex life is curtailed because they are ashamed of displays of physical affection or of making sounds in the night. A wife, particularly, feels out of place in her mother-in-law's home. Still another objection is that when a couple lives with one set of parents the other in-laws may get jealous and want to do some 'controlling' of their own."[8]

If a couple lives a great distance away, the parents may expect that the couple will use their vacations to visit them. But what if the couple has their own ideas? And what if each set of parents lives a thousand miles in opposite directions? Does that mean that each year it is a trade-off from one relative to another? If couples live relatively close to their parents, they may find greater freedom in their vacation plans. If not, adjustments and compromises need to be worked out. One compromise may be that the parents come to visit them periodically (for a previously specified amount of time).

8. Lobsenz, p. 54.

Does this factor influence your marriage? How have you worked out adjustments in this area? What do you need to do now?_____

_____

_____

5. The similarity or difference between the life-style and goals of the couple and their parents is often a source of conflict. Highly affluent, work-oriented parents who see the young couple choosing a not-so-productive life-style, or setting goals that are foreign to them, will have a difficult time restraining themselves from saying something of exerting pressure upon the couple. On the other hand, the couple could antagonize the problem by evaluating and criticizing the parents' standards.

What differences or similarities do you see in your life-style and goals and those of your parents and in-laws? Have any problems arisen over this? If so, what are you doing to resolve them? _____

_____

_____

6. Divorce can be the source of explosive

relationship problems. An ex-mate of a family member may still be considered a friend of the family. Other families or family members may still be bitter toward this person. When a young couple experiences a divorce, the children of this union are not divorced from their grandparents. In-laws remain as grandparents. And this relationship needs to be fostered and developed in spite of any hostilities. Some children in our culture have ended up with four sets of grandparents because of a divorce and remarriage. If this is the case in your life, what have you done to work out the adjustments? If you have not been divorced or married a divorced person, what would you suggest to a person who is struggling with this problem?

7. Grandchildren can become an issue with the in-laws. Some parents look forward to becoming grandparents and they have their own way of pressuring a couple to "produce." Other grandparents resent being grandparents. If the child does not look like the grandparents, is not

the sex they were hoping for, or does not behave according to their expectations, conflicts can intensify. A frequent complaint in this area is how grandparents treat the grandchildren when they come for a visit. Some have said, "When the grandchild is in my home, I'll treat him the way I want to. If I want to spoil the child, that's my privilege." Naturally, such an attitude can create dissension between families.

What if the grandchildren prefer one set of grandparents over the other and want to spend time with that grandparent and not with the other? These difficulties are really quite common. What ways have you dealt with these issues? What positive steps have you taken to enhance the relationship your children have with their grandparents?_____

_____

_____

We have been looking at the various ways that both parents and married children can contribute to problem relationships with in-laws. Let's look now at the positive factors that can be at work in an in-law relationship.

4

In-Laws Can Be Enjoyable

What about the other side of the fence? Why do many people really enjoy their in-laws? What factors contribute to a good relationship between couples and their parents? One study of 345 men and women revealed the following reasons why some couples do not have problems with their in-laws.

1. They accept me. They are friendly, helpful, and close.
2. They do not meddle, interfere, or butt into my life.
3. They are thoughtful, kind, considerate, and generous.

4. They live too far away, so we rarely see them.
5. I have no in-laws, I married an orphan.
6. We were determined to adjust. We respect each other's rights and work things out as they come up.
7. They are mature. They have outside interests and are independent.
8. They love me. We have a mutual affection and trust. They back me when I need it.
9. We are congenial and have similar interests and standards.
10. They come only when invited and do not overstay their visit.
11. They understand me. They listen and are understanding.
12. They are not demanding or possessive.
13. They are not critical, and they do not get impatient with me.
14. They do not act superior or make me feel inferior.

Go back over this list and put a "yes" by each

item that is true in your case. Put a "no" by each one that is not true at this time. Then take the "no" statements and spend time discussing with your spouse what you could do to improve these areas.

Successful in-law relationships are possible. This is not just a dream, it is a fact. To be sure, adjustments will be required and there will be times of stress, strain, tears, and hurts, but this is all part of the growth process. Too many people take a failure approach. They say, "Oh, it will never work" or "I've tried that before and it didn't work" or "They will never change." In response to these excuses it could be said that *these principles have worked in the lives of many and can for you if you are willing to try them persistently and adapt them to your own situation.* Perhaps you have tried before, but why not try again? What have you got to lose? Perhaps your in-laws will never change, but you can change or learn to live with their constant suggestions. You can learn new approaches to them to which they may adjust. It is possible!

Before you begin, ask yourself these questions: Can you communicate effectively? Are you secure in yourself? Do you have a positive self-image? Can you handle conflict? Can you be positively assertive and loving? If you can answer yes to these statements, you have the best opportunity for developing a positive relationship. If not, these areas of your life must be developed before the new relationships can have an opportunity to grow and develop. (*Improving Your Self-Image* and *An Answer to Family Communication* are two books that I have written which could help you.)

Here are some principles that you can use to improve your in-law relationships. Be sure that both you and your spouse discuss and work on these together.

1. Take a positive, optimistic view of your in-law relationships. Earlier it was mentioned that there are many stereotypes about in-laws, and many of the areas of conflict were discovered. But here is the other side of the picture. Evelyn Duvall stated:

"1. Mother-in-law is *not* always a curse; often times she is a blessing.

"2. People do *not* always find it impossible to live with or near their in-laws; many do so and like it.

"3. Men are *not* more frequently annoyed by their in-laws than are women; quite the contrary.

"4. Parents-in-law are *not* more critical of their children's spouses than the other way around; it is the younger generation that is more critical.

"5. Keeping quiet about in-law problems is *not* the only way to deal with them; many people prefer clearing up their differences as they arise.

"6. A person need *not* feel helpless about his in-law relationships; there is a great deal that can be done to make them satisfactory."[9]

2. If you are not yet married or are just newly married, you might want to consider this suggestion. When I counsel couples prior to marriage, one of the assignments I give involves their future in-laws. I ask both the man and the woman to ask their parents to write me a letter telling me why they want this other person to

9. Evelyn Duvall, In-Laws: Pro and Con (New York: Association Press, 1954), p. 313.

become their son- or daughter-in-law. The parents mail these letters to me and I read them to the couple during our last session of premarital counseling. I also ask the individuals to write a letter to their future in-laws stating why they are looking forward to having them as in-laws. Positive steps such as these have done much to build and enrich the relationships. Even at this point in your life you may want to try a variation of this idea.

3. Another important and positive step is to recognize the importance of your partner's family as soon as possible. If you have not yet married, establish friendly relationships with your prospective in-laws and try to enjoy your visits with them. Each of you will be gaining impressions of the other. Any attempts to ignore them will just increase friction.

4. Traditions! What about those ''this-is-the-way-we-always-did-it'' customs that are a part of our background and which bring some uncomfortable feelings and perhaps conflict if we are asked to change them? Who should compromise? Which family tradition should you adopt? Should the newly married couple always fit into the established family customs or should

they begin to develop their own? If everyone always goes to her parents' place for Christmas, what happens if you want to go to his parents home, or to a friend's? Do you always have pumpkin pie for Thanksgiving? What happens if you suggest a change? Who makes the gravy for the turkey dinner? And whose recipe is used for the dressing? These sound like small items but they can be major problems when they are part of the family traditions. One author expressed the conflict this way. Perhaps we can learn from her experience.

"The pressure to conform is harder to avoid with family than with friends or neighbors. You love these people, you don't want to hurt them, and you know that they are not trying to meddle, but rather include you in their lives with that same love. Jeff and I might be able to agree on new traditions for us, but how would his mother feel when we told her we'd like to have Christmas dinner alone with our children next year? Would she be hurt if we preferred to get together with the family earlier in the day or on Christmas Eve? Even if she understood that we felt Christmas morning should be spent with our four young children, would the rest of the family be as sympathetic? Would they believe that we weren't rejecting them? We wanted to share some of our time with them, but our children were at an age when teaching the rules of the Monopoly game on Christmas morning was more important than getting the turkey in the oven on time.

"Would my parents understand if we used our summer vacation to take the children camping this summer instead of spending those two weeks with them? We honestly felt it would be good for the youngsters and for us, but could they accept that explanation without reading more into it? Would my grandmother still love me if she found out that occasionally I fed my children frozen pizza?

"How would Jeff's father feel if we didn't bank where he had always banked? If we chose to reject the law firm and stockbroker he had used all his life? Would he think that we had no regard for his experience and judgment, or that we had little respect for the men he had dealt with for almost half a century? Or would he understand that we wanted younger men who might better relate to us and to our life-style to handle such matters? How would our older sisters and brothers feel if we didn't go to the pediatrician and the obstetrician they recommended? When Aunt Minnie came to visit, would we hide the frogs, pet snakes, and lizards the children took to bed with them because she'd be horrified? Or would we say, 'we're proud of our youngsters, and this is the way we choose to live.' Did we have the guts to stand up to Aunt Minnie and hope she'd understand?

"But what if she didn't understand or approve? What if none of them understood? We decided that we'd have to try to live our lives our way. We'd go as gently as we could, and tread as softly as possible through the areas that were dear to another member in the family, but go ahead we must . . . Jeff's mother, who I was convinced would be the most hurt by changes in family tradition, was the most understanding. 'You're building something good, something worthwhile,' she said, 'with your own children. Don't worry about what anyone else thinks.' . . ."[10]

10. Jeff and Jackie Herrigan, Loving Free (New York: Ballantine, 1975), 227-228. Used by permission.

You need to decide what is right for you. You need the freedom to develop your own traditions. Of course, you might decide that some of the customs from each of your backgrounds are to your liking. Perhaps you can take traditions from both sides along with some new ones which you have developed and use them for your own family. You might even introduce them to your parents and in-laws. Perhaps they can appreciate the new ideas and respond to them as you have.

5. Before you complain about your in-laws, think about this point. Have you seen many articles or books written for in-laws with suggestions on how to behave with in-laws or how to get along with them? Has your mother-in-law received some pointers on what to do or say or how to respond? Chances are she hasn't. Perhaps you or someone else could guide your in-laws to some suggestions such as the ones shared in "Guidelines for a Good Mother-in-Law," an article by Fanny Maude-Evans. Here is what she suggested:

> 1. Let the married children make their own decisions—even as to how and where the wedding is conducted and

how the children are reared.

2. Be friendly but not pushy. Treat the in-laws like you would any new acquaintance.

3. Let them make their own mistakes. Whenever the opportunity arises praise them and encourage them. Sympathize with their mistakes. Perhaps they will ask you for your advice sometime.

4. Respect their privacy, especially if you are staying in their house with them. Don't invite yourself on their outing or even trips to the store. Wait until invited. Don't expect to be included in their social life.

5. Don't put strings on your gifts. Let them decide how and when to use them, especially if the gift is money. Don't ever bring up the gift in an argument.

6. Don't criticize their life-style. We don't usually criticize friends' furniture, housekeeping habits, or cooking style.

7. Don't play "in-law soccer." Don't compete with your opposite in-laws.

8. Find and develop your new role.[11]

6. What needs do your in-laws have at this
time in their life? Quite often the reason
individuals behave in specific ways is that they
are seeking to fulfill some particular need they
have. Often their behavior does not accurately
reflect what that need is and thus we are
confused. Too often we react to another person's
behavior without considering why he is doing
what he is dong. Have you ever considered that
the suggestions coming from your in-laws reflect
some of their own needs and may not really be
attempts on their part to control or interfere?

A young woman, attending a seminar, shared
what had happened to her. Her problem was not
with her mother-in-law, but her own mother.
Whenever her mother would come over to her
home, she would constantly check the house for
dust and dirt. She was like the marine sergeant
who wore the white glove to inspect the
barracks.

11. Fanny Maude-Evans, "Guidelines for a Good
Mother-in-Law," Family Life, November 1976, pp.
11-13.

One day after this wife had worked for hours cleaning the house and scrubbing the floor, the mother came for a visit. As she sat in the kitchen her eyes spotted a six-inch section of woodwork next to the tile which her daughter had missed. As she mentioned this to her daughter, the daughter could feel the anger slowly creeping up through her body and her face started becoming tense and red. For the first time, the mother noticed the reaction to her suggestions. She said to her daughter, "Honey, I can't really be of much help to you in anything else but this is one thing that I can help you with." As the mother shared, the daughter realized that her own mother felt inadequate and useless around her and this was her only way of attempting to feel useful and needed. And now both mother and daughter have a better understanding of each other.

I am certain there are cases like this with in-laws. What we call interference and meddling is often their way of attempting to help or to feel needed. It would be far better if both parties would talk about ways to fulfill the needs of each other instead of going along for years with misunderstandings and resentments.

Most parents-in-law need to feel useful, important, and secure. They still like attention. What could you do to help them fulfill these needs? Have you ever asked your in-laws outright what you could do to help them feel useful? Sometimes you can discover this by just knowing the person, but other times it will be necessary to sit down and discuss this with the other person. It may take just a few simple actions and the expression of concern on your part to help them feel important or loved.

7. Treat your in-laws with the same consideration and respect that you would give to your friends. If your in-laws are Christians, can you see them not just as in-laws but as members of the body of Christ? Can you see them as brothers or sisters in Christ? If they are not Christians can you see them as individuals for whom Christ died? Can you remember that God's love is an unconditional commitment to imperfect people? See their potential in the same way God sees them.

8. When your in-laws show an interest in some area of your life and give advice, respond just as you would if a friend were giving you some advice. If it is good advice, follow it and

thank them for their concern. If it is not what you want to do, thank them for their suggestion but continue doing what you had planned to do in the first place. Some people reading this will say, "But you don't know *my* in-laws or *my* parents! They won't give up! They keep on and on, and if one approach doesn't work they will try another or they will try to divide my spouse and me on this issue!" Perhaps they will, but honest and firm assertiveness on your part will be helpful. They probably continue to press because it has worked for them in the past. But if you are willing to be firm and consistent, they will learn that you have the right to respond to their advice and suggestions as just that—advice and suggestions, not absolute laws.

You may have a parent or an in-law who tries to make suggestions, give advice, or criticize you in an indirect or devious manner. He makes what is known as *implication statements*. Here are just a few. You may have some of your own to add to the list. "Some sons I know call their mother once in a while." "My friend's son-in-law helped her paint her house the other day. He is so good to her." "You should see Carol's children. They are so well behaved and polite." "It's too bad that when children marry and move away so many of them forget about their parents."

These may be just harmless remarks that have no double meaning. If there is a directive behind these statements and you pay attention to it, you are just reinforcing the fact that your parent or in-law will respond in a similar manner the next time because he has been successful this time. His devious communication worked! But it can only work if you cooperate. Therefore, the best way to respond to statements such as these is to take them at face value. Don't read more into them than is there.

If he is trying to get a message through to you and you agree by saying, "It's nice that some sons do that" or "That's nice that her son-in-law was able to help her," your response will force the other person to either quit using this pattern of communication or come out and say what he really means. Either way you are helping him clear up his communication and express himself more forthrightly.

9. Keep in mind that when the in-laws seem overly concerned with your affairs, it could be that they are really concerned with your welfare

and are not trying to interfere in your life. Give them the benefit of the doubt in such cases.

10. What positive qualities do you see in your in-laws? Too often we have a habit of focusing upon the faults and weaknesses of others and overlook their positive traits. Have you ever taken a piece of paper and listed the positive qualities in that person's life? If not, take a few moments at this time and make a list. You may want to do the same for your own parents.

11. When you visit your in-laws (and when they visit you), keep the visits reasonably short. If you are there too long you may begin to get on each others' nerves. Be sure you have plenty to do when you are there. Be as thoughtful, courteous, and helpful as you can be. Consider them as you would your friends. Too often young parents walk in the door and drop the responsibility of their children on the grand-parents while they relax in front of the TV. Tempting as it may sound, resentments will develop, especially when the young mother begins to react to the way grandmother takes

care of the children.

12. Can you accept your in-laws as they are? It is very possible that you see a greater capacity for change in them because you are younger. But keep in mind that they may like to see changes in some areas of your life as well. Treat them as you would want them to treat you.

13. Your mother-in-law has been close to your spouse for many years, so recognize that the process of separation should be as gradual as possible. Give your in-laws time to adjust to the fact that you are now married.

14. If you want to give advice to your in-laws, it is usually best to wait until they ask for it. If you offer a suggestion to them, remember that it is a *suggestion* and they have the right to either accept or reject your suggestion. Do not be offended if they reject it. After all, you are asking for the very same right.

15. You and your spouse will have disagreements. When you discover that your spouse is not perfect, you may be tempted to discuss these faults with your family. Don't! If you bring these to the attention of your family you will bias them against your spouse and make it more difficult for all parties involved to achieve a better

relationship. In some cases, when a person tells his parents about the faults of his spouse, they have proceeded to call the other person's parents and complain to them, thus setting in motion a chain of events which can only lead to hurt feelings. The scriptures teach us that if we have a complaint against a brother, we are to go directly to him, not tell someone else about him!

16. Don't quote your family or hold them up as models to your spouse. He or she will probably feel defensive and seek to defend his parents even if you are correct in your statements. But why should you be quoting them or holding them up as models in the first place? If you desire your in-laws to do something different, talk with them directly. Ask your spouse how he feels about his parents. Perhaps he can share some insights about their behavior that you cannot see at this time. Remember that both families will have imperfections. This is called being human!

17. Are you protective and concerned about your own parents? Probably so. Then accept your spouse's concern for his family as well. It is very natural, normal and healthy.

18. To help you discover some of the

expectations you have in your relationships with parents and in-laws, consider these questions:

a. What do you think children expect from their parents once they are married? _____

_____

_____

_____

b. What do you think most parents expect from their children after marriage? (not just grandchildren!) _____

_____

_____

_____

c. What do your parents expect? Make a list and then put a plus (+) by the items you feel are reasonable and can be fulfilled. Put a minus (-) by the items you feel are not reasonable. _____

_____

_____

_____

d. What needs do your parents have at this point in their life? Which of these could you help fulfill? _____

_____

_____

e. What needs in your life are your parents presently fulfilling? Could your spouse help meet these needs?_____

_____

_____

Regardless of the age of your parents, they are still looking for love, honor, and respect from their children. But some parents feel their children owe them even more—obedience. It's true that while living at home physically dependent upon his parents, the child has a responsibility to be obedient. But when the child grows into adulthood and assumes adult responsibilities, he is no longer obligated to obedience. If he chooses to seek his parents' advice, carefully weighing the options before making a decision, that is to be desired and perfectly normal.

Sometimes grown children feel they "owe" their parents something in exchange for what their parents have done for them in the past. Healthy in-law relationships are built on love, and love never makes demands. The loving parent or in-law never demands love and honor, for he knows these can only be freely given. The loving relationship is not based on obligation or dependency, but seeks to give the other person the freedom to be all they can be. When your in-law relationships are lubricated with love, you will soon discover the joys that can be yours together.

5

How To Handle
In-Law Criticism

Don't be surprised when you receive criticism from your in-laws. The important thing is how you respond to them. Too many times, the people involved are either intimidated or overreact. In either case, this kind of response simply perpetuates the problem.

Here are some possible ways you can handle in-law criticism in your family.[12] The approach suggested will work in most situations. But it *will not* work *unless* you (1) know the approach

12. Adapted from John Lembo, Help Yourself (Niles, Ill.: Argus Communications, 1974), pp. 42, 43.

thoroughly, (2) put it into your own words, (3) practice what you will say several times until you are comfortable with the ideas, and (4) anticipate both positive and negative responses on the part of the other people so that you will not be sidetracked from what you want to say. You may even want to rehearse in advance with your spouse.

If someone criticizes you, stop what you are doing and look directly at the other person. By giving him your undivided attention, the irritation may be lessened.

Listen to what the person has to say. Proverbs 18:13 states: "He who answers a matter before he hears the facts, it is folly and shame to him" (Amplified). Try to hear what the person is really saying. What is behind his remarks. You may discover that you are only the object of his pent-up frustration and nothing personal is intended.

Accept the criticism as the other person's way of seeing things. From his perspective, his interpretation is correct. And he could be right, so don't write-off the complaint. If he exaggerates, don't get hung up attempting to correct him at this time.

If the one making a criticism of you asks you why you did what you did or why you do something a certain way, do not always feel that you must give them your reasons. When you give your reasons to others it puts them at an advantage as they now know where they can attack you. You could say, "I just prefer doing it in this manner," "Well, I'm not sure my reasons are that crucial; tell me more about your concern," or "Do you have a positive suggestion to offer? I would like to hear it so I can consider it and then make my choice."

Don't accuse your in-law of being oversensitive or irrational. That will only aggrevate an already delicate situation.

Don't bring up another subject or attempt to evade the present issue by joking about the complaint. It could be very important to your in-law.

Be open to their criticism and consider its possible validity before you respond. This could be an opportunity for you to grow. You might even thank the other person for bringing this to your attention, as it helps you know how the other person is feeling.

Consider the following passages in Proverbs

from the Living Bible before you make your response.

"If you refuse criticism you will end in poverty and disgrace; if you accept criticism you are on the road to fame" (13:18).

"Don't refuse to accept criticism; get all the help you can" (23:12).

"It is a badge of honor to accept valid criticism" (25:12).

"A man who refuses to admit his mistakes can never be successful. But if he confesses and forsakes them, he gets another chance" (28:13).

If you can learn to respond to the facts of what has been said instead of reacting emotionally, you will find yourself in control of the situation. For example, consider this interaction:

Mother-in-law: Oh Janice, I see that the children are outside playing and they aren't dressed warmly enough again.

(She and Janice have had a running debate over this for several years. Janice could reply with any of the following. Which would you choose?)

Janice:	Mother! They *are* dressed warmly enough. I've told you that before!
or . . .	Oh, I think they'll be okay. Don't you have something else to do?
or . . .	You feel that the children should have some more clothes on? Thank you for letting me know that. When it gets cold enough I'll see to it or I might ask you to call them in for me.

Here are some other statements which an in-law might make when visiting your home. Remember, these could be just statements of fact or they could be statements made simply for the purpose of getting a response from you.

"Oh, I see you have your refrigerator full of leftovers again!"
"You mean our granddaughter went out on a date tonight? Didn't you tell her that we would be dropping by?"

"You don't call or write me as much as you did."

Write down some typical responses that a typical young couple *might make*. Then write down some of your own responses to these statements.

_____

_____

_____

What would happen if you agreed with the other person's statement? They probably expect a defensive remark or an explanation from you. But if you don't respond in the way they are expecting, they will be forced to clarify what they are saying. Agreeing in principle with what one has said does not mean that you have changed your own opinion or beliefs. (For a detailed presentation of this approach, see Chapter 6 of *When I Say No, I Feel Guilty*, by Manuel Smith, Bantam Books, Inc.)

For example, what if Janice's conversation with her mother-in-law went something like this:

Mother-in-law: "Oh, I see you have your refrigerator full of leftovers again."

Janice: "Yes, I guess I do have some leftovers in there again."

Mother-in-law: "Well, some of them look like they have been in there for a long time."

Janice: "Yes, I am sure some of them have been in there too long."

You can see this conversation could go on for some time without having Janice commit herself to any change. There is little chance, also, that she will offend her mother-in-law.

After a person has finished sharing his complaint with you, ask him for an opportunity to respond to what he has just said. Then take the time to restate what you think the other person has told you. This does several things. First, you make certain that you have understood exactly what the other person's complaint is. Second, you are showing the other person that you take their complaint seriously and have been listening to what they have said.

When you have done all of these things, then you can share what you believe is happening. If the complaint is accurate, be sure to admit it. If the complaint is not accurate, explain why. It is also very important that you share your feelings as you present your side of the situation.

George and Margaret Hardisty have suggested some answers to four of the most common in-law conflicts and criticisms.

"My husband's parents can't forgive me for taking away their 'baby boy.' It has caused trouble.

"Most parents are willing to give up a 'baby boy' if they feel they've gained a daughter. If you haven't reached out to them with a great amount of love, going out of your way to let them know you appreciate them and generally making them feel GOOD about you, then the fault may lie in your own heart.

"One wife was so possessive of her husband, and determined to let the parents know that he belonged to her now, that she resented their calls, their visits and their questions about the children or their life. These are not healthy emotions. The couple eventually divorced. She bitterly and unfairly blamed his parents for the breakup."[13]

> "*Our relatives on both sides cause friction by cutting, unkind remarks, playing favorites with our children, being envious when something good happens to us and getting a good laugh when misfortune strikes. What can we do?*

"It is a fact of life that you can choose your friends, but you have to take what you get when it comes to relatives. You would be much better off if you lived farther away from them. Cut down on visits and get involved in something else instead: work at the church, hobbies, etc. Just don't be as available to them. Avoid using them for baby-sitters, no matter how tight your budget is.

"And why in the world are you sharing your

13. George and Margaret Hardisty, <u>Honest Questions, Honest Answers—To Enrich Your Marriage</u> (Irvine, Ca.: Harvest House, 1977), p. 175.

business with them? They don't need to know all of your misfortunes, and if it makes them envious, they don't need to know your good fortune. Blood runs thicker than water? Sometimes the best thing is to be sure there's a river running between you, with a boat available only for occasional use."[14]

> *"My father-in-law is always giving me orders. And my husband does nothing about it. This is causing much tension.*

"When I was pregnant with my daughter, we visited my husband's uncle. He kept telling me to sit down. Every time I'd move, he'd say, 'Sit down, honey.' Ten thousand times on that weekend he told me to 'Sit down, honey,' until I thought I'd never want to sit down again! If we had lived near him, I would have completely avoided him until my baby was born.

"With a father-in-law who is close by, it's different, although his motives may be the same. He probably considers you a sweet, pretty little thing that doesn't know enough to come in

14. Hardisty, p. 172.

out of the rain. Therefore he is doing you a kind turn by setting things in order. You'll have to take your stand. When he orders you to do something you don't care to do, simply say, 'Dad, that particular thing is not on my list for today,' throw him a kiss and leave the room to busy yourself doing something else.''[15]

> *"How do you handle a mother who does not want to cut the apron strings and constantly interferes in our marriage?*

"Some couples have moved to another city. It works fine, unless Mother follows them.

"Others have introduced their mother to several men and women her age, hoping to get her interested in something besides them. That works sometimes, although it's harder if she has moved in with you.

"Others encourage Mother to start baby- or house-sitting for friends of theirs. When she works, she has less time to be a bother.

15. Hardisty, p. 177.

"As a last resort, others talk it over together, decide what Mother should be allowed to be part of and what she shouldn't. Then they talk with her explaining how they feel. Sometimes she gets insulted, hurt, threatens to have a heart attack and all sorts of things, and often tries to continue right on interfering in their lives. But sometimes it's the only way to go and it is effective.

"Whatever course you take, stick with it as long as it works. Then try something else.

"Your life is your own. Mother should be allowed to visit occasionally and you should make a point of inviting her for an evening once in awhile, but the in-and-out everyday lady is too much for anyone to take. Resist talking over your problems in her presence or sharing with her if she tends to take over. If she complains because 'you didn't tell me' explain why."[16]

It would be impossible to list all of the potential conflicts couples encounter with their in-laws. However, there is no situation which cannot be conquered by a couple who are united,

16. Hardisty, p. 178, 179.

and who lovingly work at accepting and enjoying their in-laws. But it isn't always easy, especially when you encounter "push-pull" conflicts. These require an extra amount of love and understanding.

6

Push-Pull Conflicts

Different customs, traditions and life-styles deeply affect any marriage. The mixture of feelings that result is very similar to the effect that results when one person is pushing while the other one is pulling. Joseph and Lois Bird said: "We are raised in homes which have housekeeping practices, cooking styles, and family customs which differ from those of our friends and spouse, and we may grow up to believe that the way our parents did things was the right way. Christmas holiday customs are a common example. The husband may have been raised in a home in which the presents were opened on Christmas Eve, the tree was trimmed the week before Christmas, and the Christmas turkey dinner was eaten in early afternoon. His wife's family may have trimmed the tree on Christmas Eve, opened the gifts in the morning, and sat down to a ham dinner in the evening. Can anyone rationally hold that the practices of one family are 'right' and the other 'wrong'? Yet many of us do. The husband who judges and criticizes his wife's housekeeping practices, using his mother's practices as a criterion of how it *should* be done, will almost surely defeat the attainment of his goals. It's unlikely that she will immediately recognize her mother-in-law as the ultimate authority on homemaking (particularly when the issues arise over nothing more than customs). And even if mother-in-law could show her a 'better' way, she might either resist it out of resentment at having it shoved down her throat or resent her husband's implications: That she is stupid and less desirable a wife than his mother."[17]

17. Joseph and Lois Bird, Marriage is for Grownups (Garden City, N.Y.: Doubleday & Co., 1971), p. 131.

Before we consider a possible solution for this dilemma, write out what you would say and what you would do in a situation like the one above.

_____

_____

_____

If you find yourself in a similar situation, here are some suggested responses. If your cooking (or housekeeping, driving, ironing, etc.) is being compared to that of a mother-in-law, you might say something like, "Honey, one of the things that I would really appreciate and would make me feel better is for you to let me know when something I've cooked for you pleases you. I do feel hurt when I hear about your mother's cooking all of the time. I want to develop my own cooking skills but I need positive feedback from you." Or, "Jan, I would really appreciate it if you could let me know when I have done something that helps you as you work with the kids. I really become discouraged when I keep hearing about how your dad always did such and such when you were growing up." In each of these statements, you have been both positive and specific, which is the proper way to share a concern or complaint.

Daily Contacts

Another common problem is the relationship between parents who feel they must contact their son or daughter every day. For example, a wife was really bothered because of the constant mothering by her mother-in-law. Each day the mother would call and want to know how her son was doing at his job, whether he was gaining or losing weight, eating the right food, stopped smoking yet, etc. This was a situation in which the mother-in-law needed to stop making the phone calls in order for the wife to feel better. Before reading on, write out exactly what you would do or say in this situation._____

_____

_____

To resolve this conflict the partners agreed upon a goal and then communicated this goal to his mother. I suggested they say something like this: "Mom, we do enjoy hearing from you but there really is no need for you to call each day. Why don't we arrange our calls in this way. If we need something or something is wrong we'll be sure to call you. We also would like you to have the opportunity to develop other relationships and not be so dependent upon us. You know that you are always invited for dinner on Sunday. Why don't you plan to see us on Sundays and call us just on Wednesdays. That way we can stay in touch on a regular basis. In case of emergency you know you can always call." After some emotional discussions, his mother agreed and today they enjoy a warm, healthy relationship.

Vacations

Vacations can be a common problem. In some cases a spouse is irritated and comes away upset after a lengthy visit with in-laws. You may find that for everyone's sake this person should plan to engage in some enjoyable activity while his spouse visits his own parents alone for a shorter period of time. This may seem to contradict what people have been taught or what seems to be right, but if the extended stay does not promote better relationships between in-laws and does not have a positive effect upon the marriage, it may be the only solution. I am not suggesting that the spouse never visit his in-laws, but that the visits be less frequent and for brief periods of time. Many couples have found this to be an answer.

Another possible solution is shortening the entire visit. If one person would like to visit his parents for a month at the ocean and the other feels uncomfortable being there that long and being separated from his spouse for that long, compromise and make the visit for only two weeks. It might also be best not to visit in-laws or parents every year on your vacation as this creates traditions which you may find difficult to change later on. It also limits the possibility of other enjoyable vacation experiences as well.

Live-in In-Laws

The problem of in-laws living with a married couple has many complicating factors. Some are positive, others negative. The main question is: What effect will this have upon the marriage? It can cause problems in the marriage or it can enhance the marriage. When faced with this situation, a decision may be very difficult because the couple may feel that a negative decision is the same as abandoning the parents.

And yet there may be other creative alternatives that would meet the needs of the parents. You must recognize that meeting needs does not always carry with it the idea of giving others what they want. Even so, there are some couples who are able to work out a positive situation in which a parent can live with them.

If you are faced with this possibility, consider the following suggestions. Give the arrangement a three- or six-month trial. At the end of that time, determine if it is working out to everyone's advantage. If there is an adverse effect upon the children's marriage or the grandchildren, other arrangements should be decided upon. It is very important that this be agreed upon in advance and perhaps even put into writing with signatures affixed so people cannot say this is the first time they have heard about it. Sometimes, this arrangement does not work out because of the immaturity or selfishness of one of the spouses. The problem can only be corrected by some growing up on his part.

When discussing possible living arrangements with a parent, here are some questions to consider: How will this arrangement enhance our total family life? What are the possible drawbacks to this arrangement and what specifically can be done about them now to eliminate any problems? Who will be responsible for this person's meals, laundry, etc.? Will they always be included in family meals, watching TV, outings, social gatherings, etc.?

The parent living in must learn to respect the private and social life of the couple and in no way infringe upon it. Likewise the couple should not infringe upon the privacy and social life of the parent. Both should seek to encourage opportunities for growth and development.

Money

Accepting money from in-laws as loans or gifts may create problems. Often parents do this out of generosity. Other parents use this as a means of maintaining dependence or manipulating the couple. If money is ever loaned to the children or the parents, it should be done on a businesslike basis with a written contract, interest, and the understanding that both parties agree to the terms. Neither party should ever bring up the subject of the loan in a discussion in front of others, or make references to it in a family argument. There should definitely be no strings attached.

Caught in the Middle

In each of these situations, unfortunately, there are some decisions in which it seems one spouse or the other gets caught right in the middle. Most couples I know really would like to work out a compatible relationship with their in-laws—one that is enjoyable. Most couples would like to get rid of conflicts, pressures (obvious or implied), expectations, obligations, and demands. The ideal relationship is being able to relate to your in-laws and parents on an adult-to-adult basis. In some cases this is possible right from the outset of the marriage. With others it may never be possible. Some parents simply will not stop making demands, calling, giving unsolicited suggestions, and even dropping in unexpectedly.

An example of a decision that creates a strong push-pull conflict when one spouse (usually the husband) has a job offer in a different city and the other spouse's parents want the couple to stay where they are. Some of the reasons they give are, "We won't see you as much," "We can't travel as well," "We'll miss the grandchildren so much and they will miss having their grandparents close by," or "You won't be able to visit us except on your vacations." (Even that is not true! Is visiting in-laws really what you want for a vacation? What does vacation mean to you?) Many other reasons could be given but these will suffice.

Whenever a couple is faced with this kind of decision, they need to ask themselves the following questions, which were suggested by David Knox in his book, *Dr. Knox's Marital Exercise Book.*

1. With whom do you presently spend the most time—your spouse or your parents? (If you think this is a strange question, don't. Some spend more time with parents.)
2. Will you spend more time with your parents or spouse in the next six months?
3. If the decision you make is in favor of your spouse, how will this affect the happiness in the relationship between you and your

spouse?

4. If you decide in favor of your spouse, how will this affect the happiness in the relationship between you and your parents? Will it stay the same, increase, or decrease?
5. If you decide in favor of your parents, how would this affect the happiness between you and them?
6. If you decide in favor of your parents, how will this affect the happiness between you and your spouse?

The general rule here is that marriage partners usually do what increases happiness between them even if it disturbs their parents' happiness. If the parents or in-laws are disturbed by a decision which increases the marital happiness of the couple, that is the parents' problem.

The responsibility of married couples to each other involves a total commitment. This involves literally the "forsaking of all others." This not only includes in-laws and parents but friends, fishing companions, card partners, etc., for the sake of the marriage. When a husband and wife marry, they commit themselves to the task of building a good and enriching marriage. We don't usually make lifetime commitments to friends, business associates, etc., only to our spouse.

Joseph and Lois Bird suggest: "If the relationship with parents, friends, or relatives— their visits, actions or influence—has a negative affect on our relationship with the one person to whom we have committed ourselves, we can make no rational choice other than to curtail—or even terminate—contacts with our parents. The responsibility rests on each one of us. If necessary, we may have to take steps which could alienate our parents, and they may be deeply hurt.

"But we aren't suggesting a decision to hurt one's parents or friends, which would, in any case be irresponsible. We are saying we must make choices for our marriage, not against anyone.

"We could try to chronicle all the arguments, the special circumstances, the excuses we employ to avoid a painful responsibility, but rational thinking is ruthless in cutting away our escapes. And if the reader attacks these questions realistically—and maturely—he will do his own cutting, painful though it may be.

"Should we love our parents? By all good reasoning, yes. But in the ways which we can, ways which are compatible with our primary commitment: Marriage."[18]

One husband handled the demands of his own parents with persistence. He and his wife Mary were sitting at home when the phone rang. Jim's mother was calling.

Mom: Hello Jim, this is Mom.

Jim: Hi Mom, how are you doing?

Mom: Oh, all right I guess. (She sighs.)

Jim: Well, fine, but how come you're sighing?

Mom: Oh, well, I guess I haven't been doing too good. I don't know what's wrong. Anyway, are you coming over this weekend? I was hoping to see you. You know it's been several weeks since you and Mary have been here.

Jim: I'm sorry you're not feeling too well, Mom. No, we won't be coming over this weekend. We have some other things that we have already planned to do.

18. Bird, pp. 142, 143.

Mom: Well, what's more important than seeing your dad and mom? Aren't we important to you anymore?

Jim: I can understand that you want to see us, Mom, and you are important, but we won't be coming over this weekend.

Mom: Well, we sure are disappointed. We were positive that you would be over, and I already have a turkey for dinner. Did you know that?

Jim: No, Mom, I didn't.

Mom: Both your father and I are disappointed. Here we were expecting you two to come and we have the turkey already bought.

Jim: Mom, I can see that you're disappointed, but we won't be able to be there this weekend.

Mom: You know your brother and sister come over to see us all the time. We don't even have to ask them!

Jim: That's true Mom. They do come over more and I'm sure they are a lot of company. We can plan for another time and work it out in advance.

Mom: A good Christian son would want to see his parents more often.

Jim: What about my not coming over makes me a bad Christian son?

Mom: If you really loved and cared for us you would want to come and see us.

Jim: What about my not coming to see you this weekend means I don't love you?

Mom: It just seems that if you did, you would be here.

Jim: Mom, not coming over does not mean I don't care for both of you. I love you and Dad. But I won't be there this time, I'm sure you can use the turkey now or freeze it. Now, let me check with Mary and look at our schedule and see when we could all get together.

Perhaps this kind of approach seems foreign to you. Jim was persistent and did not allow himself to be manipulated. He shared with his mother that he did love her. If she chose not to believe him just because he did not come over, she would have to learn to accept and live with that problem. Perhaps in time, if Jim continues to be firm and loving, his parents will learn a new way of responding to him.

What should you do if you have a definite problem which needs to be brought to the attention of an in-law? First, be sure you and your spouse have discussed it and worked it through yourselves. Unanimous agreement is the ideal, but you may experience some situations in which you are the only one who feels as you do and you may have to work out the solution by yourself. Here are some guidelines [19] to follow when bringing a problem to the attention of another person. Remember there is no foolproof method for deciding with absolute certainty the correct approach to take with conflicts. These are only suggestions which should be adapted to the problem at hand.

It is important that you identify the situation that is a problem. You need to examine your own attitude, feelings, and responses to see if you are perpetuating the problem or contributing to

19. Adapted from Lembo, pp. 40, 41, and from H. Norman Wright, Communication and Conflict Resolution in Marriage (Elgin, Ill.: David C. Cook Publishing Co., 1977), pp. 11, 12.

it in some manner. Assuming that others always create problems intentionally is faulty thinking. The other person may not be aware of the conflict. If he says he was not aware of it, believe him. Give him the benefit of the doubt. This is the way a trust relationship can be developed in the future.

Rehearse in your own mind exactly what you plan to say before you confront another person. Visualize your words and manner of communication. Work out in your mind alternate choices and determine your own needs. Then visualize forgiveness, understanding, and reconciliation.

Do you have to be angry in order to get your point across to others? Some people don't seem to respond unless anger is a part of the message. But when you share a complaint or a criticism with another person in a calm, well-thought-out manner, it will always bring about more change than if you respond in anger.

Many people find healthy problem solving to be a major area of dissatisfaction in their in-law relationships. Here are a few techniques which will help you avoid an angry explosion.

1. Recognize conflict issues early. No one has to look for conflicts, but if a disagreement

arises, accept it as an opportunity to gain understanding of yourself and the other person. Consider it a time of growth. Your attitude toward the problem will determine the outcome. Your pessimism or optimism will influence conflict resolution.

2. As soon as you can, verbalize the problem or complaint. The longer you let a problem fester, the greater the possibility of resentment and bitterness eroding the relationship.

3. Share your problem or concern in private so you don't embarrass the other person or cause him to feel that he must save face.

4. Select the most appropriate time. (See Proverbs 15:23.) It is very important to select a time that will allow for the greatest understanding and cooperative effort.

5. Let the person know that you are pleased with several aspects of the relationship before sharing what it is that bothers you.

6. Use "I statements" such as "I feel" and "I don't like to be" rather than "you are" and "you did this." "You statements" sound like accusations and quickly lead to self-defense and nonlistening, and perhaps even to counter-complaining.

7. Pinpoint the actions that concern you. Don't try to be a mind reader by focusing on what you *think* the other person's motives are. Perhaps he was rude or didn't listen, but you don't really *know* that he definitely planned to do that.

It is often very helpful to put your feelings down in writing. This will produce a much better understanding of the entire situation, especially how the problem relates to unfulfilled needs. As you describe the problem in writing, be sure you consider both your own and the other person's behavior, along with the circumstances that surround these behaviors. Carefully define how you understand the problem. Then attempt to look at the situation from the point of view of the other person. How might they define the problem? As you write, you may discover some of the real issues involved that you may have overlooked before. The more narrowly you define the conflict, the easier it will be to resolve the problem.

8. Identify your own contribution to the problem. In resolving a conflict, your approach must be "We have a problem." Even though you believe you have not contributed to the

conflict, the way you approach the other person and the words you use will affect the potential resolution. When you are willing to accept some responsibility for a problem, the other person perceives a willingness on your part to cooperate and will be much more open to working together towards a solution.

As you consider what you are going to say to the other person, keep in mind these practical steps:

• Choose one word that best indicates what you want to talk about.

• State the word or subject you want to talk about in one complete sentence. Be precise and specific. Try not to blame, ridicule, or attack the other person. Do not overload him with too much information all at once.

• Take responsibility for the problem. Tell the other person why you are bringing this matter up for discussion. For example, "I have a problem. I have something that is a little difficult for me to talk about, but our relationship is very important to me, and by talking about it I feel that we will have a better relationship. I feel that ___ is the problem, and this is what I am contributing to it: _ _ _. I need to hear what you think and how you feel about it." This is an example of a very healthy way to express yourself in what otherwise might be an explosive confrontation.

If your partner approaches you in this manner, respond by saying, "Thank you for telling me. If I understand what you feel, the problem is_ _ _. I can agree that you feel this way." Restate the problem to make sure you have correctly understood your partner.

9. Comparing this person's actions and behavior with the failings of others does little to help solve the problem you are concerned about.

10. Forget the past. Talk about the present issue without making reference to past difficulties.

11. Deal with only one complaint. It is too easy for the other person to feel dumped upon if he receives a barage of problems all at the same time.

12. Suggest in a nonangry, nondemanding, nonjudgmental way some of the realistic solutions that could be implemented.

13. Allow the other person to share his

feelings and ideas about the problem. If he responds in anger to what you have said, his response is no reason for you to become angry.

Remember, a valid complaint always has two characteristics. It should be specific and positive. Statements like, "You're always complaining about something," "You always make comments about my housecleaning," or "You always seem to interfere when we are disciplining the children," are negative and nonspecific. Here are some examples of positive and specific complaints which will elicit a more constructive response.

"I would really appreciate your sharing some positive things about what's going on with you."

"When you have a complaint, I would really appreciate it if you would also suggest a positive alternative or solution."

"When we are disciplining the children, I would appreciate your not saying anything about what we are doing in front of them. I am always open to positive suggestions, but please share them with me later when they are not around.''

You really don't have to be caught in the middle. You can eliminate much of the pain of a push-pull conflict by honestly asserting to the other person your feelings and reactions. If done in a spirit of love and concern, the results can be constructive.

7

Building
Better In-Law Relationships

It's time to check-up on yourself. What are you doing to build better relationships with your in-laws? To help you evaluate yourself, write out your response to these questions:

1. What have you done in the past to let both your own parents and your in-laws know they are important to you?

2. During the past two weeks, what have you done to express your positive feelings toward your parents and your in-laws?

3. What new things could you say or do that would let your parents and your in-laws know they are important to you?

_____

_____

4. Describe what you have done to discover from your parents or in-laws what kind of relationship they expected from you and your spouse? (Such as how often to visit or call, their involvement in disciplining your children, etc.)_____

_____

What can you do about this in the future?

_____

_____

5. In the past how have you helped your parents or in-laws meet their own needs and develop a greater meaning in life?

_____

_____

How can you help them in the future?

_____

_____

6. If your parents or in-laws have had difficulty

in the past, how did you respond to them?

How can you be more helpful in the future?

7. In the past what have you done with your parents or in-laws to make it easier for them to demonstrate love towards you and your immediate family?

How can you improve this in the future?

8. What have you done in the past to assist your parents or in-laws to receive love from you? What have you done to demonstrate love to them?

It would be so much easier if engaged couples would spend some time discussing their impending in-law relationships rather than attempting to bring about changes later on. After patterns have been set and expectations established, attempts of change can be very difficult. *But change is possible if people are willing to pursue their newly established goals.*

A "Do Plan"

If you desire a change in a relationship, perhaps you could begin by establishing what has been called a "Do Plan." This approach always focuses upon positive behavior and positive changes. In implementing this plan you do not look at the behavior of your in-laws, you begin by looking at your own behavior. Look at yourself, for you can only control what you do, not what others do. Because you are younger than your in-laws, you also have greater flexibility when it comes to making changes. It would be nice if your in-laws would make any necessary behavioral changes. But if they cannot, it is up to you to learn new ways of responding to them or decide not to see them as much.

In creating your plan, first ask yourself if what you are doing in response to your in-laws is really helping you and the relationship. Don't be concerned about the past or the future right now, just the present. If you find that some things are not really helping you, select a small area of your life in which you would like to change. It is crucial to write down what you want to change and the way you go about making this change. What you write down must be detailed and specific. Do not leave anything to chance.

Again it must be emphasized that your plans must focus only upon the positive. Negative plans will not work as well. For example, if you often get into a quarrel or argument with your in-laws when you see them, don't write in your plan, "When I see my in-laws I will not argue or quarrel with them." It would be better if you would say, "When I get together with my in-laws I will be friendly and warm, and ask them positive questions." If your in-laws usually drop in unexpectedly when you are not prepared for them, call them and arrange for a specific visit that would fit into your schedule. This approach would convey a message to them and allow you to have better control of the situation.

Substituting a definite planned approach for a negative behavior is one way to build better relationships. It can also be effective in

implementing scriptural teaching in relationships as well.

As you plan new approaches to others you will
find that some of these new behaviors lend
themselves to developing a routine. This is
important if you want to break old habit patterns.
If you can continue to write out your plans,
implement them frequently, and discuss them
with your spouse, they will stay fresh in your
mind.

One couple visited their in-laws or was visited
by them only once a year because of distance
and travel expense. But beginning two weeks
prior to their visit the couple spent several hours
planning how they wanted to respond to their
parents and in-laws. They rehearsed ways of
responding to what they knew might arise as
minor irritations. The visits were always
enjoyable.

In your plans it is important that you see
yourself as the active person. Success does not
hinge upon what any other person does.

Your plans should be specific, the steps
involved small, and the purpose reasonable.
And there must be some value and purpose in
bringing about this positive change.

8

What Kind Of An In-Law Are You?

In our discussion to this point, we have considered the other person as an in-law. But if you have in-laws, then you are also an in-law yourself. What kind of an in-law are you? To find out, here is another "quicky quiz" for all mothers-in law, fathers-in-law, sons-in-law and daughters-in-law.[20]

1. Do you insist that your in-laws see you often? If you do, are your requests made clearly or are they implied indirectly?
2. When your relatives choose something that is not your choice, do you take it as personal rejection?

20. Adapted from Hardisty, pp. 180, 181.

3. Do you drop in on relatives unexpectedly? If you do, what kind of reaction do you expect? What kind of reaction do you usually receive?
4. Do you let your children know when you feel they are not rearing your grandchildren properly?
5. Do you complain to other relatives about your in-laws.
6. Do you give lots of advice even when others don't ask for it?
7. Do you probe for family secrets?
8. Do you often take sides in family quarrels? If you do, why?
9. Do you write frequently? Do you expect your in-laws to write as often as you do?
10. Do you have many friends other than your own relatives?
11. Do you accept your in-laws with love and not criticism?
12. If you have recently been critical of any of your in-laws, was your evaluation of that person objective or subjective?
13. Did you consider the preferences and wishes of both families when you planned your wedding?

14. Do you habitually look for the best in your in-laws? Do you tend to tell your family and friends about the good qualities you see in your in-laws?
15. Have you and your spouse grown together enough so that you can speak of *our* families rather than of *my* family and *your* family?
16. Do you make decisions before consulting other members of your family?

As you've read through these questions and thought about your answers, it would be good to go one step further and discuss them with your spouse. See if you agree in your evaluation of yourselves.

Now let's go one step further and see how well you can apply your ideas to some very real in-law problems. Here are four case studies. Read over each situation and then answer the questions that follow each one. Again, it would be helpful if you discussed your reactions to each case study with your spouse and even with your in-laws.

CASE STUDY #1

Wife: "If my mother-in-law makes one more comment on my cooking or my housekeeping, I think I will go bananas! She has nothing else to do so she drops in at least three times a week to criticize my menu, tell me I should use a different furniture polish, explain why the plant won't grow in that corner, and what a waste of money it is to have Henry's shirts done at the laundry.

"She *never* has anything positive to say. Everything that comes out of her mouth is either a direct or an implied criticism. I keep telling Henry he'd better shape her up, but he just says I'm too sensitive. At least he agrees his mother can be a pain some of the time, but then he tells me I'm a big girl and I can fight my own battles."

1. If she stopped talking at this point and asked for your advice, what would you suggest to her? _____
_____

_____

2. What do you learn about this woman by what she says? _____
_____

_____

3. Who should deal with the other?
   How would you go about getting that
   person to talk to her?_____

_____

_____

CASE STUDY #2

" 'Arthur's mother is our major problem,'
Lucille told the counselor. 'He is tied to her
apron strings—but tight. I tried to be very nice
to his mother when we were first married. But
she never did like me. Infact, one time she came
right out and told me that she didn't believe that
I was the right woman for him and I never would
be.

" 'The truth of it is that his mother spoiled
him badly. She waited on him hand and foot. She
was from an old-fashioned family, and she got
all of her satisfaction from cooking and
housekeeping. I don't keep house very well, and
I admit it. But she didn't have to come over and
pick things up after me like she did. It made me
so mad I screamed at her and told her to get out.
And do you know what, Arthur didn't even take
my side!

" 'As a matter of fact, I think that's what hurts

the worst. I can sometimes abide his running over there all the time, but I can't stand the fact that he doesn't stand up for me. He never says anything to his mother in my defense. He never talks back to his mother at all.

" 'His mother keeps working on his emotional system, even more so now that his father has died. She makes him feel like he ought to come and see her every day. He goes over there at least seven or eight times a week. If I try to make him promise not to, he just lies to me and goes anyway. I've caught him at it.

" 'I want to move away from his mother. He went and bought a house about a block from her place last year. I almost left him then.

" 'One time when we were first married, he took a good job down in Atlanta. Do you know how long we stayed down there? Two months! He just couldn't stay away from Mama. He'll tell you all sorts of reasons why we came back: It was a poor job, we didn't like the area, his boss was impossible to work with, but those aren't the real reasons at all.

" 'Actually, I don't get along any too well with my own mother. At least, though, I always know where I stand with my own mother. When I do something she doesn't like, she tells me about it right there and we can fight it out. But his mother—she just looks hurt and tries to do even more things around *my* house. It's infuriating. Last month I forbade Arthur to let her come around any more. And I made him promise again that he wouldn't go down there. I want you to tell him, too, that he has to stay away. If he doesn't, I'm going to get a divorce. And I mean it.'

"Arthur said, 'Lucille is frantically jealous of my mother. She doesn't even want the children to have gifts from Mother. Lucille is younger than Mother, and she could at least try to understand how Mother feels now that her only son and her husband are both gone. Lucille could end this marriage problem anytime she wanted to by just acting decently to my mother. But she won't.

" 'Lucille is a terrible housekeeper. I think she'll tell you that herself. And really, that's part of the problem. Lucille knows she should pick things up, but when Mother came over here and did it, she began to boil. That's really what started all the trouble.

" 'I know Lucille says she wants me to take her side, but what it amounts to is that she wants me to punish my mother as a demonstration of my love for her. She has said it almost that way. What am I supposed to do, castigate my mother because she's trying to help? I can't do that. I've tried to make things as easy as I can for Lucille. I used to ask her to go with me to Mother's, especially on the holidays. But now I don't even ask anymore. Every once in a while I take the children by myself. And then does Lucille scream! She says my mother tries to condition the children against her. Actually, all Mother does is give them a little loving care that they rarely get at home.

" 'Anyway, I don't go down to Mother's so much myself anymore. Actually, Mother has been a big problem for me all my life. Since I was the only child and her only real interest, she expected a lot of attention from me. I know I feel obligated to help her, especially since my father died. Who else is there? You just can't tell her to curl up and die. But Lucille doesn't understand this. Her own mother is an independent type who can take care of herself. She tells Lucille off regularly, and Lucille seems to respect her for it.

" 'I don't know what I'm going to do. My life is miserable this way. Lucille wants me to move way across town, and in some ways it might be a good thing, although I would never admit that to her. On the other hand, it might just increase the time I had to be away from home, because I know I can't ever abandon Mother altogether.' " [21]

1. Write down what you see as the main problem. Can you identify it in one word? What other problems does it create?

_____

_____

2. Who is contributing to the problem and in what ways?_____

_____

_____

3. What are five possible solutions and who should implement them?_____

_____

_____

21. Klemer, pp. 278, 279.

4. What biblical teaching would help resolve these conflicts?_____

_____

_____

5. Have you ever experienced this? If so, how did you feel? How did you resolve it?

_____

_____

_____

CASE STUDY #3

" 'If Tony would only try, he could get along with my mother,' Lisa told the counselor. 'But all he does is carry on about how "that mother of yours isn't going to tell me what to do." The funny thing is, she really doesn't try to tell him what to do. But he's gotten so used to fighting with his own mother about whether he's old enough to do this or that that he thinks he has to do it with mine. The slightest thing she does to help us seems to offend him. She bought some cute new clothes for the baby last week. But as soon as Tony found out who they came from, he took them back to the store. He said he could provide for his family and didn't have to be beholden to anybody.

" 'I don't mean to say that Mother is always right and Tony is always wrong. She gets in a little dig at him every once in a while about how he ought to grow up. That just makes matters worse. Then there's no living with him for a week.

" 'But Tony's so sensitive that sometimes Mother doesn't have to do anything and there's trouble. He never has gotten over something that happened the first week we were married. I became seriously ill, and Tony took me to the same hospital where I had been a student nurse. When my mother heard about my being so sick she rushed over to the hospital, too.

" 'While I was being diagnosed, they wouldn't let either Tony or Mother see me. After they figured out that I had peritonitis, the director of the nursing school, who knows me well and who had been in the emergency room with me, went out to the lobby where Tony and Mother were. He was looking out the window and Mother was on the other side of the room. The director knew my mother, but she didn't know Tony, so she went up and told Mother about my condition. Tony got all upset and told them both off right there. He said he was the one who was supposed to take care of me.

" 'That incident should be almost ancient history now, but it isn't. Tony still carries on about it. Now my mother has gotten angry, and she won't come to see us anymore. I don't know what I'm going to do. I'm caught right in the middle.'

"But Tony had a different story. 'Lisa is so dependent on her mother that she can't see what's going on,' Tony told the counselor. 'Her mother influences her in a lot of subtle ways that I don't even think she realizes. She goes over to see her mother, and her mother tells her what we ought to have or how I ought to behave. Then Lisa comes home and tells me we need so-and-so or you ought to do such-and-such. I know what we need, and I know what I ought to do. Her mother is worse than my own ever was about trying to manipulate me.

" 'The worst part about it is that it's so insidious that Lisa doesn't see it. Her mother says to her something like, "I don't want to tell you how you should do it, Lisa, but I know that when your father tried to take advantage of me sexually, I just got my doctor to tell him that I wasn't strong enough to have sex more than once a week." I actually overheard her tell Lisa that. Now what do you think of that, Mr. Counselor?

" 'It's getting so I'm not the boss in my own home. Last week she and her mother went shopping, and when they came home she showed me a new coat she had bought. I didn't like it, and I told her so. But her mother said to her, 'It's beautiful and it fits you so well.' I made such a fuss that she finally took the coat back. But she didn't want to.

" 'I'm not going to put up with this much longer. Either we move away from mother or else out I go.' ' '[22]

1. Write down what you see as the main problem. Can you identify it in one word? What other problems does it create?

_____

_____

_____

22. Klemer, pp. 281, 282.

2. Who is contributing to the problem and in what ways? _____
_____
_____

3. What are five possible solutions and who should implement them? _____
_____
_____

4. What biblical teaching would help resolve these conflicts? _____
_____
_____

5. Have you ever experienced this? If so, how did you feel? How did you resolve it?
_____
_____
_____

CASE STUDY #4

" 'We moved in with Georgia's father about two years ago,' Craig told the counselor. 'At the time it seemed like the only thing to do. Georgia's mother had just died, and there was no one to care for her father, who is a partial invalid. You wouldn't know there's anything wrong with him to hear him talk, though. He's fiercely independent. But I guess he does need someone near in case of an emergency. Besides, we need to save money, and he had a very big house. It was just about the time I had realized that the only way I was going to move up at the research laboratory was to go back and get a master's degree. All in all, moving in with her dad looked like a real good thing—then.

" 'But as soon as we got in the house, trouble started. Something seemed to come over Georgia. She stopped doing the housework when her father wasn't around. Now she never does anything around the house unless she's absolutely forced to. I'd like to help with the dishes and the housework, but if I do, she lets me take over completely. If I try to talk calmly with her about it, she flies into a rage.

" 'Sometimes she trys to compete with me like a little child. If I point out to her that we don't have enough money for some of the things she's bought in the last few weeks, she'll say, "Well you spent money on yourself last month; now it's my turn to spend some on me." She doesn't want me to give in to her. Apparently what she wants is a kind of a forceful dominating man like her father used to be. He told her what to do and she loved it. She talks to me about how everything should be fifty-fifty, but she really doesn't mean it. She wants the security of having a husband who is sometimes authoritarian and who is always self-confident. I'm not that way and I admit it.

" 'But her father is, or was. She still looks to him for leadership. Whenever there is a decision to be made, if I try to talk it over with her she says, "We'll ask Daddy." If I try to tell her what to do, then she sulks and I know she runs to Daddy after I'm gone. It isn't that the old man doesn't try to stay out of it. He knows there's a problem, too. But she nags and digs him until he tells her off, and then he tells her exactly what she should have done in the first place. Almost always it's just what I said, but she takes it from him and won't take it from me.

" 'Georgia is quick to criticize me, but she gets petulant and stubborn when I correct her. I don't mind her pointing out my goofs to me in a good-natured way when we're alone, but it sure fries me when she mentions some mistake I made in front of her dad. That's what most of the fights have been about in the last few months.

" 'I told her a week ago that we're going to move out of that house. But now she insists that the old man needs us more than ever. He doesn't need Georgia; she needs him. She apparently won't leave, and I guess I'm not forceful enough to make her. She says if I go, I'll have to go by myself and she'll keep the child. What can I do?'

"Georgia agreed to almost everything Craig had said. 'Yes, it's true,' Georgia said. 'I do trust Daddy more than I trust Craig. But that's because Craig takes such stupid positions sometimes. I can see now that it's often because he wants to make me feel like he's a leader like Daddy was. But somehow he just hasn't got the personality for it. I want him to be the leader—desperately I want him to be the leader—but I want him to show me that he's the leader by accomplishing things. And he needs to prove himself not only for me but for himself, too. He always feels as if I'm comparing him, and I guess often I am.

" 'Now that Daddy is old and not so forceful

anymore, I feel sort of lost. I guess really I'm looking for something I had a long time ago. This is a bad situation. I know we should get out of the house now, but I just can't bring myself to go. My father really does need me. But there's more to it than that. I have always felt completely accepted by him even when he was punishing me. When Craig criticizes me, I just get mad. Sometimes I get mad enough so that I wish Craig would leave.' ''[23]

1. Write down what you see as the main problem. Can you identify it in one word? What other problems does it create?

_____

_____

2. Who is contributing to the problem and in what ways?_____

_____

_____

3. What are five possible solutions and who should implement them?

23. Klemer, pp. 279, 280.

_____

_____
_____
_____

4. What biblical teaching would help resolve
   these conflicts?_____

_____
_____

5. Have you ever experienced this? If so, how
   did you feel? How did you resolve it?

_____

_____
_____

9

How One Couple
Worked It Out

The ongoing process of marital adjustment involves both the development of your relationship with your spouse and the changing relationship with your parents. Both aspects are interwoven. That is why it is so important to discuss as early as possible—even before the wedding—what kind of relationship both you and your spouse want to have in the future with your in-laws.

Here is an example of how Tom and Susan dealt with their future in-law relationships concerning the frequency of family visits. [24]

24. Adapted from Walter Imbiorski and John Thomas, Beginning Your Marriage (Chicago: Delaney Publications, 1972).

151

Each heading can be a guide to your own discussion. Space is provided following their comments where you can write in the particulars about your own situation. Work together with your spouse on this project.

A. First, consider the real issues involved:

- Our relatives would like us to live close and visit together frequently.
- We want to maintain contact with our parents. We have good positive feelings towards them.
- We want to be careful that we are not smothered by them or get trapped into visiting patterns that we will be expected to maintain for years.

Write down some of the issues involved in YOUR situation:

_____
_____
_____
_____
_____
_____

B. Describe how you feel about these issues:

Tom:

- I really don't mind going over to visit her folks. The food is good. Long visits tend to be boring.
- My family is not as close as hers, so I enjoy the warmth of her family.

Susan:

- His family is rather cool towards each other. His mother can be critical or nosey at times, and this makes me angry.
- I think his family has some unreasonable expectations for us, but I don't know yet how to bring this out into the open.

How do you feel about the issues in YOUR situation:

YOU:

_____

YOUR SPOUSE:

_____

_____

_____

C. Describe some of your expectations with in-laws:

- We love and respect our parents so it is fitting that we maintain a good relationship.
- They loaned us money and we are grateful.
- Our children need grandparents.
- Tom's mother tends to be overly possessive and we want to avoid that type of relationship. We want her to treat us as mature adults.

Describe some of YOUR expectations:

_____

_____

_____

_____
_____
_____

D. Which spouse has more at stake in any decision regarding in-laws:

- Susan is the only daughter of a doting
  father, so she may risk hurting him if we
  don't visit often.
- Tom is one of nine children and his parents
  enjoy having us visit, but their interests
  are spread over all the children. They
  probably would not be hurt by less
  frequent visits.

What is at stake with your in-laws:

_____
_____
_____

E. As you live with your decision, who will take
the brunt of the consequences:

- Both of us.
- Susan will get a lot more flack on the telephone from my mother and sisters if we don't visit often and regularly.

What about YOUR decision:

_____

_____

_____

F. What qualities do you admire in others that you wish were stronger in you when faced with these kinds of situations:

- I want to be firm, yet loving.
- I don't want to back down.
- Sometimes I am being manipulated and don't know it until later. I want to be aware of what is happening while in the situation.

What qualities do YOU desire in your situation:

_____

_____

_____

_____

G. Taking all these factors into consideration, what conclusions can you make about the decisions you face:

- Our visits to our in-laws need to be irregular and flexible.
- We want to do more than just sit together and watch their TV.
- We will make no individual decisions without first talking it over together.

What conclusions can YOU make:

_____

_____

_____

_____

An important factor to remember is that any relationship is an on-going process. You never arrive at your objective, but are always working towards your goal. In your relationship with your in-laws, and within your own family, two interesting games are available to assist you in building communication and relationships. They are the *Ungame* and the *Social Security* game. It's amazing how people can feel a sense of closeness and warmth playing games together. Try it with your in-laws!